The
Home Schooling
Father

The
Home Schooling
Father

by
Michael Farris

BROADMAN
&HOLMAN
PUBLISHERS

The Home Schooling Father
© 2001 by Michael P. Farris

All rights reserved
Printed in the United States of America

Published by
Broadman & Holman Publishers
Nashville, Tennessee
First published in 1999 by
Loyal Publishing, Inc.

0-8054-2587-X

1 2 3 4 5 6 7 8 05 04 03 02 01

Dedication

I dedicate this book and myself to my children:
Christy, Jayme, Katie, Jessica, Angela,
Michael Jr., Emily, Johnny, Joey, and Peter.

Contents

1. Spiritual Leadership Is Not Optional 9

2. Helping Your Helpmeet 21

3. Fulfilling Your Role as Protector 35

4. Preparing Your Child for a Career 45

5. Preparing Your Child for Marriage 69

6. Preparing Your Child for Citizenship 91

7. The Treasure at the End of the Road 113

Chapter 1

Spiritual Leadership Is Not Optional

*A*ll Christian fathers need to exercise real spiritual leadership in their families. In home schooling families, the need for spiritual leadership is particularly acute. Home schooling fathers who fail to provide reliable spiritual leadership are asking their wives and children to fight a Spiritual Revolutionary War without power or weapons.

There is little reason to wonder why a Christian father would want his children to be home schooled. Home schooled kids can read. They can write. They can think. They have deeply ingrained moral and spiritual values. They can get along in a family setting. Home schooled children can "socialize" with children of all ages as well as with adults. As a general rule, a home schooled child will make an excellent worker, spouse, parent, and citizen. Home schooling works.

Parents do not need professional training to become excellent home school instructors. But they do need divine empowerment if they are going to have the stick-to-itiveness necessary to keep to the task for the long years as their children progress from toddler to adult.

There is much talk about "burnout" in home schooling circles. While good academic advice has its place, the only real defense against burnout for the Christian home schooling family is God's mighty power. Academic strategies deserve only a passing reference in building a defense against burnout. The Holy Spirit is no mere academic counselor. He is the indwelling person of the Trinity who can unleash the power of God Almighty in your life. Ask any weary home schooling mom. She doesn't need advice. She usually knows the right thing to do. She simply needs the power to perform what she already knows she should do.

Every home schooling father needs to begin to examine his duty to his wife and children by considering their need for spiritual empowerment. They are going to be mocked by friends, neighbors, and relatives. They may be prosecuted by the authorities. They are going to face spiritual warfare. They are going to have to do a lot of plain old hard work.

Fathers do not have the job of directly supplying the spiritual power their families need. That is God's job. But a father has the responsibility to see to it that God's power is flowing freely to each and every member of his family. A father is to serve as the family "pastor," providing spiritual leadership for his home.

Home schooling holds greater potential for spiritual success than any other form of education. Satan knows this fact as well. He will not willingly let your home schooling thrive. The forces of darkness do not want children to be raised who can not only read and write, but also reason biblically and conduct spiritual warfare through godly family living. Every father should realize that his family needs his spiritual leadership in increased measure once the decision to home school has been made.

In other words, Dad, if you want your children to be home schooled, you must commit yourself to becoming a vital spiritual leader for your family.

In real life, few Christian homes have any measure of spiritual leadership from Dad. Slipshod mediocrity is the rule in the homes of most born-again fathers. The vast majority of these fathers are dynamic, effective leaders and workers on the job. But things are different, a bit more laid back, at home. The sad truth is that a lot of dynamic business leaders are lackadaisical spiritual leaders.

Let me get real with you at this point. I am a better spiritual visionary in public than I am a spiritual leader at home. There are many things that I will share with you in this book that I can validate with good success in my own life. There are a good many other things, however, with which I am still struggling.

Recently I stumbled onto my wife's prayer journal that she has kept for years. It was very humbling to realize that for a number of years her number one prayer request was "Make Mike the spiritual leader of our family." I know I have made at least some progress because this request is somewhat lower on her prayer list in more recent years. But I think you get my drift.

Sometimes Christian authors and speakers give the impression that they have mastered the ideas they are sharing with the audience. There is a reluctance to share personal weakness for fear that the audience will conclude that the spiritual principles being taught don't really work.

The audience sees it differently. They see these spiritual principles as unattainable because they are being propounded by a person who appears to be living close to spiritual perfection. Audiences tend to get demoralized by apparent spiritual perfection and consequently lose any hope of mastering the principles for themselves.

Spiritual leadership is simply too important to you and your family for me to cause you to stumble on the stone of my false perfection. It is critical to our mutual success that we, reader and author, assume we are going to strive together to attain the goals which God has for each of us. I have learned some of the lessons in this chapter and in this book. There are other lessons I am still learning.

Home schooling is growing rapidly because of a phenomenon I have called the "Great-kid-average-parent" syndrome. People look at the kids produced by home schooling and say, "Those are great kids! I'd like my kids to turn out that way." Then they look at the parents and say, "Those are average parents. If they can do it, I can do it too."

In a similar manner, by writing this book I am committing myself to a high degree of public accountability to do a very responsible job of being the spiritual leader of my own family. I trust that my example will provide encouragement to my fellow "average" dads. If I can raise spiritually successful children, you can too!

The Goals of Family Spiritual Leadership

A father is usually expected to provide spiritual leadership by (1) taking his wife and children to church with him; (2) praying regularly for his wife and children; and (3) conducting regular family devotions. Most Christian fathers attain only the first of these goals with any consistency.

There is no doubt that we should routinely discharge all three of these duties. I recently realized, though, that these tasks are simply *methods* of family spiritual leadership, not *goals*.

In fact, when we focus on these three duties rather than on attaining spiritual goals, these duties tend to become distasteful tasks to be endured—the spiritual equivalent of home maintenance projects.

My desire to discharge these duties has been recently invigorated by a new focus on the spiritual goals I have for my own children. I now see these duties as a means to a desired end, rather than a mere responsibility that must be discharged.

This shift in focus came as the result of teaching an adult Sunday school class on training families. I suddenly realized afresh that, as a father, I have a responsibility to make sure that my children are spiritually prepared for adulthood when they leave my home. The fact that I have two teenagers rapidly approaching adulthood has no doubt served to crystallize my thinking as well.

The parents in this class and I began to share the spiritual goals that we had for our children. Before this none of us had ever stopped to make a list of such goals. We realized that we were likely to reap vague spiritual results as a consequence of our failure to have a clear set of spiritual goals.

We discovered that another benefit of having clearly defined spiritual goals was to make possible meaningful assessment of how we were doing. It also became possible to map out specific plans for our children's spiritual training and development.

No army general would ever try to train soldiers in the haphazard way we try to train children. The army has an organized plan and a training course of increasing rigor designed to produce soldiers capable of winning the battle. Our duty to train our children is no less important. It is equally necessary for us to develop goals and plans for the training of the spiritual soldiers whom God has entrusted to us.

Our class identified twelve spiritual goals that we want to make sure that our children attain before they leave home as adults:

1. My child will be sure of his or her salvation.
2. My child will love and understand God's Word.
3. My child will know and willingly obey God's rules of right and wrong.
4. My child will be maturely walking with God.
5. My child will know his or her individual spiritual gift(s) and call from God.
6. My child will be able to teach spiritual truths to others.
7. My child will be an effective witness.
8. My child will spend daily time with God.
9. My child will have a servant's heart.
10. My child will be self-disciplined.
11. My child will be in fellowship and under the authority of a local church.
12. My child will understand the power of prayer.

When I examined this list 1 realized that there were several of these goals which my older children had already attained. But I also realized that some of these important goals would slip through the cracks in the busy years of adolescence if I didn't make a planned effort to ingrain these characteristics into my children's lives.

There are other spiritual goals you could identify for your children. This list is not intended to be exhaustive. It simply illustrates the kind of goal-setting that is critical to spiritual leadership.

In short, then, spiritual leadership requires a father to:

1. set spiritual goals for his children,
2. plan activities and training designed to inculcate these goals, and
3. periodically assess his child's progress.

Fathers who have fuzzy spiritual goals for their children will raise spiritually fuzzy children.

The Methods of Family Spiritual Leadership

You may be currently frustrated with your attempts to plan meaningful spiritual activities for your family. Once you have set spiritual goals for your children, it is easier to plan activities since you will need to make specific plans to reach specific goals. If you want your children to spend daily time in God's Word, then you need to plan activities that are designed to reach this goal. If you want your children to be effective witnesses, then you need to plan activities that will give them an opportunity to witness. They need to see you witnessing. They need to see the value of witnessing. And they need to see witnessing from God's perspective.

For years I tried to encourage my older children to spend daily time in God's Word. I tried to model regularly this behavior for the kids by having my own time in God's Word. I gave them verbal encouragement to have their own daily time. Sometimes I praised them for doing a good job. Sometimes I chastised them for irregularity. But they were typical Christians—they were not faithful every single day.

Then around Christmas of 1988, I had an idea. I told my three oldest children (those old enough to read) that if they read the Bible every single day in 1989 I would pay them $100 each. If they missed one day of reading I would deduct $25. There would be a deduction of $10 per day for every day missed thereafter. Christy, Jayme, and Katie each collected $100 on January 1 the next year.

We have continued this practice and our children continue to faithfully read their Bibles every day. Christy is now seventeen. She recently told me that I didn't need to pay her anymore because daily reading of her Bible had become a habit she thought would last for her whole life. She didn't feel she needed a material reward because she understood the spiritual value of a daily time with God.

Her response was one of the spiritual highlights of my life in terms of raising my children. She gave me solid evidence that my goal for her has truly been ingrained in her life. She reads the Bible every day because she wants to hear from God, not merely because Dad has asked this of her.

The methods you use to inculcate a spiritual goal will, of course, vary according to the goal in question. Financial or material rewards are not always appropriate. In general, you can use one or more of the following methods to encourage your children's spiritual development:

1. Model the desired behavior.

If you want your children to know the value of prayer, for example, they need to see you pray. You need to give them the opportunity to see God answer your prayers. When answers come, be sure and take the time to praise the Lord and remind your children that God really answers prayer.

2. Give instruction.

Spiritual goals originate in Scripture. Make sure that your children obtain foundational instruction in the Word for each of your goals. Again using the prayer example, you should teach basic scriptural truths about prayer to your children.

3. Give an opportunity to participate.

Your children should be given opportunities to pray both privately and publicly. It is equally important to give your child an opportunity to share answers to his or her prayers.

4. Give vision.

Giving your child only the rules, e.g., "You should pray," is insufficient. A child who is taught only rules will eventually either burn out or reject the teaching. Children need to be given spiritual vision. They need to understand the importance of the spiritual goal. They need to see the value of this goal in their own lives. They need to see this goal from God's perspective.

5. Assess progress.

This simply means checking up on your child. The only method of checking up that makes any sense in this context is to sit down with your child and review things with him. Find out what he is doing and how he feels about it. This time gives you invaluable opportunity to reinforce teaching and vision.

Family devotions, church attendance, and regular prayer for your children still need to figure into your plans and activities. Many fathers have a difficult time determining what they should do in family devotions. Once you have established specific spiritual goals, family devotions become a lot easier to plan. You can use family worship time to emphasize the specific spiritual goal you are working on at the time.

Having spiritual goals and plans is not an absolute guarantee of success. But if you have no goal, you will hit it every time.

The steps of action required of a spiritual leader are not that different from the kind of leadership men are required to demonstrate on the job. We fathers need to exercise at least as much diligence in our spiritual goal setting, planning, and review as we do on our jobs. After all, the stakes are a lot higher.

God is the ultimate foundation of all our endeavors. However, from the perspective of human responsibility, your spiritual leadership is the foundation upon which your home schooling program will be built. You want your children to succeed, so give them a foundation for spiritual success. Be a real spiritual leader.

Chapter 2

Helping Your Helpmeet

*T*he plain truth is that moms do the vast majority of the work in home schooling. As dads we are asking our wives to take care of housework, cooking, laundry, childcare, *and* teaching our children. That is a *lot* of work.

As we have already noted, a home schooling mom may begin to feel "burned-out" if she is carrying this load alone. There are two principal solutions to burnout: (1) reliance on the Holy Spirit and (2) a dad who helps. Let's discuss each of these solutions in some detail.

Moms and Dads Must Rely on the Holy Spirit

First, moms and dads alike need to realize that utter dependence upon the Holy Spirit for strength and guidance is a critical factor in home schooling. Any Christian who tries to undertake this responsibility in his or her own strength invites burnout. "I can do everything through Him who gives me strength" (Phil 4:13). Not every home schooling mom is going to have a husband to help her. Some moms are married to unbelievers who give only tacit support to home schooling. Dad could be called into the military and mom could be left home in the States to teach the kids while he fights to defend the country. And a lot of dads travel in their jobs. Because of these factors, many moms face periods of time when they are bearing the responsibility of the children's education alone.

For some moms, this situation is permanent. There are a number of courageous single moms home schooling their children. They may have been divorced or widowed. Others are pragmatically "single moms" when it comes to home schooling because their husbands are simply unable or unwilling to help year after year.

Moms who face this task alone, whether temporarily or permanently, need to remember that Jesus Christ is available to be their strength. He will be a husband to the widow, a father to the fatherless. He alone is ultimately sufficient to meet our needs.

The need for reliance on God may be more pronounced when a mom faces home schooling all alone, but the truth is that all of us need to rely on God's strength in order to do God's work. We may be able to fake it on our own for a while, but in the end successful home schooling is dependent upon successfully learning our need to depend on God.

Dads Must Help

The second solution to burnout is a father who is committed to helping his wife with the task of home education. Some dads may ask themselves, "Why should I be focusing on helping my wife? I thought she was supposed to be *my* helpmeet."

A quick review of the allocation of scriptural responsibilities for the training of our children supplies a ready answer to this question.

Many of the verses which give the command to teach our children are not specifically directed at either parent:

> *These commandments that I give you today are to be upon your hearts. Impress them on your children. Talk about them when you sit at home and when you walk along the road, when you lie down and when you get up. Tie them as symbols on your hands and bind them on your foreheads. Write them on the door frames of your houses and on your gates.*
>
> Deut. 6:6-9

Train a child in the way he should go, and when he is old he will not turn from it.

Prov. 22:6

However, whenever the Bible directs a child-training command to just one parent, that command is directed to fathers:

Fathers, do not exasperate your children; instead, bring them up in the training and instruction of the Lord.

Eph. 6:4 (See also Psalm 78:5–6;
Proverbs 4:1; 13:1; Isaiah 38: 19; Joel 1:2–3.)

In fact, even in passages which are not explicitly directed at either parent, such as Deuteronomy 6:6–8, the cultural setting of the command clearly implies that the duty to teach children is primarily the duty of the father.

Therefore, a father is not really being asked to assume a portion of the wife's responsibility when he is asked to help with home schooling. He is simply being asked to do at least a portion of his own job himself rather than delegating the job entirely to his wife.

How to Be Helpful

Some dads teach one or two of their children's academic subjects. Others help tutor when a child has special difficulty.

Others help their wives grading school papers. Some help with decisions on curriculum choices.

Because of work schedules or personal limitations, some dads are unable to help with the academic side of home schooling. Some dads do the laundry. Others assume a greater-than-usual share of the routine cleaning responsibilities. Some fathers take on extra amounts of childcare for younger kids in the evening so Mom can plan and correct schoolwork.

There is a multitude of different ways to achieve the goal of helping your helpmeet. You may find it helpful to change tasks from year to year. The specific task you perform is not as important as the emotional commitment to your wife that is communicated by your acts of helpful service.

Your wife needs to know that she is not home schooling alone. She needs to know that you view this as a team effort and that you are willing to help her shoulder the tremendous responsibility that is involved in home education.

Sit down with your wife and discuss this with her. Let her do most of the talking. Find out how she is doing with the levels of responsibility. Determine where she needs the most help. Discuss ways your help would be the most meaningful to her.

One of the things I do with my wife is to serve as an objective observer to help her analyze problems she experiences with our home schooling. After one such discussion, I was able to plan a daily schedule for her that solved a number of the conflicts in organization she was having teaching our oldest five children while having to watch our youngest three children.

(Here's the answer we have found to this common problem: Our oldest three children each take a forty-five minute childcare shift in the morning. The little ones all take naps in the afternoon. Thus for two hours and fifteen minutes in the morning, and the bulk of the afternoon, our little ones are not in the way of Vickie's efforts to teach. This program was greatly improved when I later suggested that our older children start teaching reading readiness, math readiness, music, and physical education to our preschoolers during each of their sessions. Each of our older girls teaches one or two subjects based on her own interest and ability.)

The two biggest areas of pressure for your wife are academics and household chores. You need to help share the load in at least one of these areas. By discussing your family's needs with your wife, you will be able to come up with a plan that suits the schedule and abilities of both you and your wife.

Beyond the areas of academics and household chores are a number of other things you should consider in meeting your responsibility of helping your helpmeet.

1. Give her a break.

Before we began home schooling, my wife would plead for intellectually stimulating discussion when I came home from work at night. She had been with little kids all day and wanted her mind to function on a different level for at least a few minutes a day. Generally, I was dog tired and wanted simply to sit and vegetate.

Home schooling now provides my wife with a great deal of intellectual stimulation. And the level of stimulation has increased each year as our oldest two girls work their way through high school. She is now discussing Shakespeare and other great works of literature on a regular basis. She has plenty of intellectual stimulation.

Now when I come home at night we both want to sit and vegetate. Unfortunately, we have eight little people who need live parents, not two couch potatoes.

Although the need for "stimulating" conversation has diminished, my wife still needs mental breaks from her responsibilities. Just as you need to leave your job and do something else for a while, your wife needs some mental breaks from her heavy responsibilities with your children.

My wife takes a walk for about forty minutes every day. In good weather and bad. In sickness and in health. In fact, she is out walking usually within two days after giving birth. Her walks are the most cherished part of her schedule. When our kids were younger I had to be home for her to be able to take the walks. Now that we have teenagers, she is able to walk in the late afternoon after her teaching responsibilities are through for the day.

Another home schooling mom in our church loves to swim. They have younger children, so a couple of nights a week, Dad watches the kids while mom goes to the park department's indoor pool and swims laps.

A regular mental break, even if it is just for thirty or forty minutes, is a great source of comfort to home schooling moms. Dads will need to provide the opportunity for their wives to be able to do this.

Beyond the daily type of breaks, you should strongly consider some longer breaks for your wife.

For a period of several months, my wife and I went to Wendy's on the same night each week to simply talk— mainly about issues related to our home schooling and how we could better work together. This was very successful for a long time until a new responsibility took away our established night.

Take your wife out to dinner at least twice a month— even if it is only for fast food. There's nothing that says you have to eat fast and leave.

Another type of break we have tried is weekend trips together. We try to do this about once a quarter. For the last few years our trips have usually been in connection with my appearance at a home school convention. However, we have been able to take some short trips alone without any outside responsibilities.

Because my wife has nursed our children, many times we have taken the baby with us. But when you have eight children, it is still a tremendous break just to have only one child with you.

One very special time for us came when I "had" to attend a religious freedom meeting in Paris. (I am on the international board of a Swiss-based human rights organization, Christian Solidarity International.) Thanks to United Airlines' frequent flyer program, I was able to take my wife and oldest daughter with me—all of us flying free. This trip was a very good break for my wife and at the same time gave us the opportunity of a lifetime to spend time alone with our oldest daughter before the years slip past and she is gone.

You don't have to go to Paris. (Unless you can fly for free and get free conference accommodations—then you really must go!) One of our favorite times was when we went to a hotel in a neighboring county and simply spent a day and a half alone.

When it comes to giving your wife a mental break, the old saying "a little goes a long way" has great applicability.

2. Be the leader in discipline.

When you are away at work, your wife obviously has to take on the responsibility of disciplining your children. And I trust that you have jointly discovered that it is generally a bad practice for your wife to tell your kids, "Wait until your father gets home." She needs to apply immediate, consistent discipline contemporaneous with the wrong behavior.

However, there is a good application of the phrase "Wait until your father gets home." Your wife deserves to "pass the baton"—or shall we say "pass the rod"—to you upon your arrival. When Dad is home, he needs to bear the primary responsibility of administering discipline in the family.

There are several reasons for this. First, the administration of discipline is one way to communicate who is in charge. Children intuitively know how to work one parent against the other. They ask Dad and if Dad says no, they ask Mom to see if they can get a different ruling.

(Incidentally, we have a rule about this in our house. If they have already asked one of us, the other parent always affirms the decision already given. And if they appear to have deliberately tried to do an end run around an unwanted decision, they get punished.)

By having Dad clearly in charge of discipline, there is greater stability than where there appears to be two people in equal authority. The Bible says that no man can serve two masters. This principle is true for your children. They need the assurance that comes from having Dad clearly in charge when he is at home.

Moreover, your wife will most likely welcome the relief. Child discipline is not pleasant. You often have to sort through various tales by quarreling siblings. You have to decide if a child is telling you the truth. You have to determine appropriate levels of punishment. You have to discern if some kind of restitution is warranted.

All of these steps take a lot of mental energy. And your wife has played the role of detective, prosecutor, judge, and jury enough times during the course of the day to be good and ready to let you hold night court in her stead.

Discipline is a prerogative of leadership. If you are not in charge of discipline, you are not the spiritual leader of your home.

3. Pitch in when you are tired.

Most men come home from work dog tired. The modern nightmare of commuting exacerbates the fatigue coming from normal work. Some jobs are more physically taxing: some are more mentally or emotionally draining.

The last thing most fathers want to do when they get home is to jump right in and begin helping with the children and the household duties.

Most home schooling moms have reached their level of physical and emotional fatigue around dinnertime as well. The level of work involved in a home schooling mother's day is as taxing both physically and mentally as most men's jobs. Mom is tired too.

Home schooling dads look forward to arriving home to relax. Home schooling moms look forward to dad's arrival so she can get some help. These conflicting expectations are likely to result in clashes.

Dads are likely to feel entitled to a little rest and relaxation because they have worked hard all day. But dads need to look at the situation from their wife's perspective as well.

There are solutions to this problem. And finding solutions will necessitate some give and take from both husband and wife. But the key to the solution is the father's attitude: If Dad communicates an overall attitude of willingness to help, he will set the foundation for a team spirit that should exemplify the Christian home schooling family.

The wife's responsiveness and flexibility is important, too. My wife has learned to read my levels of exhaustion. Recently, I came home from a very important meeting that lasted a lot longer than expected, it did not go well, and ended in a drive home that was an hour longer than normal. Vickie let me sit and vegetate that night. But when I come home from a more normal day's work, she has justified expectations that I will help out.

Usually the most helpful thing I can do is to take our youngest children and keep them occupied while Vickie finishes dinner. Just playing with the little kids can communicate a great deal of compassion for your wife's burden of responsibilities.

A home schooling wife has a tricky problem. She needs to be able to communicate appreciation for the hard work her husband has performed all day for the benefit of the family. And she also needs to be able to deliver the message that she needs help. She needs to use delicacy in communicating her need for help. Her call for assistance could be stated in a way which says, "It's about time you showed up. I need some help around here. You haven't done a single thing here all day while I have been wrestling with these kids." Such a message shows total lack of appreciation for the husband's contribution to the family.

But at the same time, a husband whose usual pattern is to never help when he arrives home because he is tired also shows a total lack of appreciation for the wife's contribution to the family.

If you help when you are tired—especially during the first hour when you arrive home—you will reap the reward of a wife who feels loved, appreciated, and a part of a team.

4. Don't neglect spiritual leadership.

There is no need to repeat the substance of chapter 1. But let's take another quick look at the issue of spiritual leadership from the perspective of your wife.

Before coming on full time with Home School Legal Defense Association, I worked for six years as General Counsel for Concerned Women for America. I attended a lot of conferences for women and had considerable opportunity to gain insight into the trends of thinking among Christian women.

Nearly every Christian woman believes that the number-one need in her family's life is for her husband to exercise genuine spiritual leadership. I know my wife certainly feels this way.

The husband's spiritual leadership builds a strong foundation for every family—but especially for the home schooling family. Your wife is more than willing to do her part in helping to do a major share of the "finishing work" in the course of building your "spiritual home." But her job is much more difficult if she is trying to build without a proper foundation.

Nothing you or I can do to help our wives is more important than providing a strong foundation of spiritual leadership that unleashes the power of the Holy Spirit into the lives of our families.

Chapter 3

Fulfilling Your Role as Protector

*T*he frontier father knew his role. He kept his rifle handy, was trained in its use, and was constantly ready to protect his wife and children from all attackers.

Home schooling is a frontier-type movement and home schooling fathers need to be prepared to fulfill a role exemplified by fathers of this prior age. Home schooling fathers are called upon to defend their families against attacks by public school officials and other government agents who resist our expansion into what they perceive to be their territory.

I have been providing legal defense for home schooling families since 1983. I have handled thousands of phone calls for help, intervened in hundreds of legal conflicts, and appeared in courts dozens of times. It is my sad duty to report that the vast majority of my contacts with home schooling families have been with home schooling *moms.* This is the same report I get from the other attorneys who work with me at Home School Legal Defense Association.

When the truant officer comes to a family's door, we usually get a call from Mom. If officials send a letter threatening legal action, normally we hear from Mom. We recognize that Dad is often at work during the hours where it is necessary to contact an HSLDA lawyer. But there have been dozens and dozens of times I have experienced the following scenario: I return a phone call to a family needing legal assistance. Even though the father answers the phone, he immediately turns the call over to the mother since she is "handling the home schooling."

Families are, of course, free to allocate responsibilities in whatever manner they deem best. And in our modern society it is politically incorrect to portray fathers as protectors and mothers as needing protection. Those who choose to live by modern philosophy may also choose to disregard this advice. However, if a family is attempting to live by the biblical pattern, then the father's responsibility to protect his family is clear. It is inconsistent with the biblical notion of the husband as the head of the home for a father to force his wife into the role of legal protector.

Christian Dad, you must, therefore, take the lead in defending your family if there is legal conflict with your home schooling. When mothers are pushed into this role by default, there is a tendency for her to become overly fearful and sometimes unnecessarily hysterical. Mothers tend to react this way because they are being forced into a duty that the Bible assigns to fathers.

As lawyers, we are often required to fully explain the possible consequences of pursuing certain courses of action. Sometimes these potential consequences are fairly severe. But we always try to reassure the family that no HSLDA member-family has ever lost custody of its children, no parents have ever been convicted of truancy and then sent to jail, and no family has ever been effectively ordered to stop home schooling. A mother forced to be the family's "protector" sometimes overreacts to an explanation of the legal possibilities. Logic dictates that their families will likely weather the legal storm just like all the other families that have preceded them. Mothers are more than capable of being logical. I never attribute a mother's overly anxious response to any failure of the mother; rather, I believe that this is simply a natural response when a father fails to be his family's protective leader.

There are three things you, as a father, need to do to fulfill your role as the legal protector of your family's home schooling program: have a legal plan for your home school, take the steps of action to complete the legal requirements for home schooling, and take the lead in resolving any legal difficulties which arise. Let's discuss each of these responsibilities in turn.

1. A father needs to have a legal plan for his family's home school.

It is an unfortunate reality, but every home schooling family needs to recognize that they must deal with legal issues affecting home education. This does not mean that you need to fear anything. Rather, it simply means that you need to have a plan which adequately addresses your family's legal needs. These are the minimum components of a legal plan:

a. Obtain a copy of your state's home schooling law.

You should endeavor to obtain a copy of your state's law or a reliable legal explanation of this law in layman's language. If you are familiar with the use of a law library you can obtain a copy of the state home schooling law. In approximately thirty-four states, this would be fairly easy to do since the law is relatively straightforward and found in a single place in the law books. In the balance of the states, however, you really need to know more information than is easy for a layman to obtain. In some states you would need to find specific provisions within the private school laws. In other states you would need to find the court decisions which have judicially declared the right to home school.

The easiest way to obtain proper information is to write or call Home School Legal Defense Association. HSLDA will send you a free copy of a one-page summary of the law in your state. This summary contains all the appropriate legal citations so you would have the necessary information if you wanted to do the law library research on your own.

b. Clarify your family's spiritual beliefs concerning obedience to the law of your state.

Many Christian families have faced legal requirements which give them serious pause about their ability to obey both God and man. Do not lightly determine that you cannot obey your state's home schooling law. You must be able to point to specific principles in Scripture which would preclude you from obeying a specific legal requirement. It is not enough either legally or spiritually to say that "I don't want to obey the law today because it might change tomorrow and ask me to do something I don't want to do. In Matthew 6:34, Jesus tells us to let today's troubles be sufficient for today. And the courts will tell you that you cannot get constitutional protection from a reasonable law which is on the books today just because you fear that the government may impose an unreasonable law tomorrow. If you conclude that the government is currently requiring you to do something God forbids, then you should have constitutional protection for your refusal to obey. Unfortunately, the courts are not often generous in acknowledging your rights in such situations, but if correct constitutional law prevails, you should win.

c. Make a plan for your family's potential need for legal defense.

HSLDA spends between $750 and $10,000 on outside legal expenses in the defense of our cases. This does not consider the fact that our staff lawyers do the vast majority of the work in almost every case. If our internal costs were included, the true cost of defense would be between $2,000 and $100,000. Obviously, these latter amounts are incurred only in the rare cases that work their way through the appellate courts and on up to the United States Supreme Court.

Few families can afford these kinds of expenses. Home School Legal Defense Association is the only organization that guarantees you full legal defense. We pay all attorneys fees and court costs including expert witness fees, transcripts, and travel. The membership fee is $100 per year. There are other organizations which will defend home schooling families—sometimes for free—but these organizations take only selected cases and are limited by the amount of money which can be raised through direct mail fund-raising techniques.

Obviously, I think the wisest course of action is to join HSLDA. When thousands of families stick together for our collective defense, we have the ability to come to the aid of any single family who is targeted for prosecution by the educational establishment.

2. A father needs to take the steps of action to complete the legal requirements for his family's home school.

It is very important for you to have a legal plan before you ever make contact with any school official. Far too many families attempt to comply with the home schooling law before they have made a plan, and end up in unnecessary trouble. HSLDA will not accept into membership any family already in legal trouble.

If you know your state law and have an adequate plan for defense, then you are in a position of strength for dealing with government officials.

A related principle is this: You should not simply fail to make a decision about your legal situation. You need to make a deliberate decision whether or not you will comply with the law and then promptly execute that decision. There are a few states—but only a few—in which the best course of action is to simply wait and see what happens. At times the best decision is to make no contact with the government. But that is the best decision only if it is deliberately made. A decision based on procrastination is never appropriate.

There are a number of states with real deadlines for filing home schooling notices. If you do not have a biblical reason for non-compliance, you need to take the prompt steps necessary to meet those deadlines.

3. Fathers need to take the lead in resolving any legal difficulties which arise.

You cannot and should not expect your wife to interface with government authorities for the protection of your home school, at least if you subscribe to the Bible's teaching about the husband being the leader of the family. Interaction with authorities is a leadership duty and squarely falls on the father's shoulders. You should make the phone calls to government officials. You should sign any letters to officials. (It is okay to have both parents sign such letters.) We had to defend one case in which the mother alone faced criminal charges simply because she had been the sole signator on a letter to the school district.

You should also be the primary contact with HSLDA or other legal counsel. Your wife can be your conduit if your work situation will genuinely not allow you to deal with lawyers during the day. But she will know the difference if you have dumped the entire responsibility on her shoulders. You should be the leader of this team effort. You should neither abandon your wife nor fail to consult with her to make sure you both are in agreement on every major step in a legal encounter. I urge you to exercise loving leadership and teamwork. Be neither a wimp, nor a tyrant.

Other Ways You Can Protect Your Family

Difficulties with extended family. Your family's home schooling may face difficulties other than with legal officials.

Your wife and children may be ridiculed by members of your family. An unfortunate number of home schooling families report serious conflicts with members of their extended families.

If members of your family disagree with your home schooling, they should quickly learn that any such discussions need to be with you or at least include you. It is never appropriate for relatives to "hassle" children over a decision made by their parents. If you learn of such an occurrence, you should promptly (and very politely) inform such a relative that your child is not responsible for this decision—YOU are—and that any questions or comments should be directed to you.

If it is your wife's family that is the source of difficulties, she will usually want to be present in any serious discussions. That's fine. But I would strongly recommend that you should also be there and lovingly take the final responsibility to explain your decision.

Protecting your family's schedule.

People will attempt to take advantage of your family because of your home schooling. Mothers from your church who have preschoolers will want to drop them off at your house so that they can go shopping. As your children get older you will find (as we have) that many people will try to get your older children to come baby-sit for them during the school day. You should help your wife and children to establish rules for your family that prevent such interruptions.

You will obviously want to bend the rules to help with true emergencies, but you should judge an emergency by a standard you would use to justify leaving your job.

Another great interrupter of your family's home schooling is the telephone. Buy a telephone answering machine, make sure it works, and use it.

Chapter 4

Preparing Your Child for a Career

Good directs both fathers and mothers to teach their children: "Listen, my son, to your father's instruction and do not forsake your mother's teaching" (Prov. 1:8). I believe that both Scripture and God's design in nature teach that mothers have a special relationship with children of tender years: "...but we were gentle among you, like a mother caring for her little children" (1 Thess. 2:7). At the other end of childhood, I believe that fathers have special responsibilities to prepare their children for adulthood. Obviously, neither parent has exclusive duties with younger or older children. Both parents need to be involved throughout the child's life. But fathers do have special responsibilities as a child approaches maturity. This chapter and the two which follow delineate these special responsibilities.

Fathers have a duty to see that their children are properly prepared for a career. When children are at home, the father has the clear biblical mandate to be the provider. God never intended for children to receive lifelong provision from their father. God intended that somewhere along the line, fathers would stop simply giving their children a fish and teach them how to fish for themselves.

Jesus was trained by his father to follow his trade of carpentry. When Jesus called James and John to be his disciples, they were in their father's boat working as fishermen (Matt. 4:21-22).

Since that time there has been a universal understanding in Western civilization that a father has the responsibility to properly prepare his son for a career. Today, this responsibility extends to our daughters as well. For those who want to follow biblical instruction on the special roles for men and women, there are additional considerations which we will discuss later.

There are many facets of your responsibility to train your children for a career. The first step is to teach your child good work habits.

Teaching Your Child to Work

As president of HSLDA, I have responsibility for about thirty employees. As we interview potential workers, we have found that there are four qualities which are becoming increasingly scarce. These qualities should be emphasized in children from the youngest ages on up to prepare them to become good workers when they are adults.

1. Respect for authority.

Employers want workers who will respect the principles of a chain of command and who will cheerfully receive a directive as an order. Too many workers believe that their supervisor's directives are merely suggestions which can be followed or not, depending on how the employee feels about the matter. Others will do what their supervisor asks but only with a begrudging attitude. A worker who is willing to follow directions with a smile will shine as a star in the eyes of any employer.

This is an attitude which home schooling fathers must instill in their children. If we fail to teach our children to obey, they will never follow directions on the job. If we are tyrants and obtain obedience through undue harshness, then our children will probably become the kind of workers who do what they are told—and no more—and with a sullen attitude.

We need to teach our children to joyfully obey and genuinely respect those in authority over us. Our willingness as fathers to display respect for authority in our own lives is a critical factor in helping our children develop a proper attitude toward authority. Do you show a proper respect for your boss? Do you have a good attitude toward the leadership of your church? What do you say about traffic policemen in the presence of your children? How do you talk about the president and other political leaders?

You can respect those in leadership without having to agree with them about everything. If you disagree, you should model the practice of a respectful appeal for your children. If your governor supports a gay rights bill, for example, calling the governor bad names in front of your children will not instill the kind of attitude you desire in your children. Instead of bad-mouthing, write a strong letter of appeal to the governor and let your children read it. You should then pray for your governor to change his mind. And since the political context allows us to change those in authority over us, you should work diligently to get a better person in office the next election.

2. Taking initiative.

As an employer, I always value a person who not only does what he is told, but sees something else which needs to be done and does it. Taking initiative is a skill and attitude which is much easier to develop as a child than as an adult.

If your child is told to wash the dishes, he has the opportunity to show initiative if he not only washes the dishes, but also sweeps the floor. A child who learns to walk into a room, see a problem, and resolve it will climb to the upper echelon of any business.

For those rare children who naturally take initiative (we have one child out of eight like this), you simply need to heap on the praise and not take them for granted. Most other children need to be taught how to take initiative, how to anticipate needs, and how to see needs that others will realize only later and resolve them right now. Then they need opportunities to put these lessons into practice.

Household chores are the best possible training ground for learning to take initiative. If you have to tell a child to feed the dog every single night, that child has not learned to take initiative. He needs to learn to do the task without being asked. If your toddler makes a mess in the kitchen (hypothetically speaking, of course), your ten-year-old should learn to bend down and clean it up and not just step over it.

3. Striving for excellence.

Too many in our society have forgotten how to be excellent. We are satisfied with being "good enough." When we were in school the prevailing practice was to produce "acceptable" papers. Now the prevailing attitude on the job is to produce "acceptable" goods and services.

I want my children and all home schoolers (indeed, all children) to learn to strive for excellence. There is a real temptation in the home schooling community to be satisfied with a standard that is less than excellent.

Recently, I talked with a mother who was upset because her sixteen-year-old son was being denied the right to take the G.E.D. He had taken the practice exam and was achieving scores in the low 50s in each subject area. He needed a score of 45 on each of the subjects to pass. The average public high school graduate scores a 50. I told the mother about her legal rights, but then told her I wanted to take off my lawyer's hat and talk to her as a home schooling father. I strongly encouraged her not to view her son's ability to pass the G.E.D. exam as a signal that she should quit home schooling him. Passing the G.E.D. is simply not a sign of academic excellence. I encouraged her to keep on working hard until her son had reached a level that would far surpass that of the average high school graduate.

Albert Shankar, president of the American Federation of Teachers, America's second largest teachers' union, has repeatedly said that 75% of the public high school graduates are functionally illiterate. Beating a functionally illiterate student by a few points on the G.E.D. is no cause for great rejoicing.

We need to go beyond being "good enough" in home education. Our children should learn to read, understand, critique, and judge literature. They should have a thorough introduction to some of the great books of literature. Our goal, for example, should be to raise a child who can read, understand, and evaluate literature at the level of skill necessary to master Charles Dickens classic, *A Tale of Two Cities.*

Our children should also be able to write well. Children should do two things to learn to become excellent writers: (1) read a great deal of excellent writing, and (2) practice, practice, practice. It is not enough for our children to be able to write clear prose. We should teach our children to write logically and persuasively. I find a good many people willing to express opinions. Few, however, know how to provide logical written support for their opinions.

Our children should master basic math and be able to understand and perform some advanced math. Not every child needs calculus. In fact, very few truly need this level of math instruction. But the ability to perform algebra and geometry are benchmarks of acceptable mathematical performance. These two courses are also excellent methods for teaching logic and reasoning. My ninth grade algebra teacher taught me skills I frequently use now to analyze a proposed piece of legislation. Logic, orderly thinking, and reasoning skills are important in many fields outside of the traditional careers associated with math.

There is one academic subject in which we need to go far, far beyond public school standards. We need to provide the best available instruction in the history and geography of our nation. While the public schools are drowning children in the academically meaningless and morally damaging world of "multiculturalism," we should be teaching our children to thoroughly know the history and philosophies of the men and women who founded this country. If American children are not taught the principles of freedom, America will not be free for very long.

I had the very unique privilege of receiving a double dose in the principles of freedom. First of all, I learned them from my father. He regularly would talk with me about the things going on in our political and legal world. He exposed me to men who were well schooled in the issues of the day. But it was primarily my father's own discussions about current events and explanations of the relation of historical events to the current problems that shaped my early thinking.

Then in the later years of high school, and especially in my first two years of college, I was taught a "different gospel." I came home from college my freshman year and proclaimed to my father that I thought that "Christian humanism" was the best philosophy. I also began to spout political views which were moving rapidly to the left.

In my junior year in college, I was turned around in a single week by a professor of constitutional law. Dick S. Payne taught me the principles of freedom by teaching me the original intent of the Constitution. His course returned me to the political philosophy my father taught me and from which I have not strayed in the last twenty years.

In order to teach my own children the same principles that I was taught by Dr. Payne and my father, I recently wrote a high-school-level textbook entitled *Constitutional Law for Christian Students*. This book is being used by over 2,000 home schoolers and is one way to make sure that our children are truly excellent in the understanding of our Constitution and system of government.

Academic instruction is not the only area in which we should strive for excellence. As we discussed in chapter 1,we need to lead our children to spiritual maturity. In *every* area of life we need to encourage our children to do everything they do as unto the Lord—with excellence.

4. *Willingness to work hard.*

There are too many lazy people. Go to a shopping mall and try to get a clerk to help you. Go to any fast-food restaurant. Chances are you will encounter mostly lazy people—people who have no enthusiasm for work.

Let me tell you a secret. I am a lazy person by nature. I do not like to work. It is true that I am very busy and work long hours for Home School Legal Defense Association. It is true that I help my wife with the home schooling of our eight children. It is true that I do a lot of work around the house. (My wife says I do at least "some" work around the house.) It is true that I am an elder in my church, and for a year and a half I pastored my church on top of all of my other responsibilities (as a volunteer). I coach a softball team, chair an international human rights organization, do a daily radio program, and write books. Nonetheless, I remain a lazy person *by nature.*

Obviously, something happened to me along the way to adulthood that allowed me to overcome my natural tendency toward laziness. That "something" was my father. He taught me to work. And I have to admit it was over my extreme protests. I fought him every step of the way. I developed some of my best argumentative skills trying to talk my dad out of some work projects he wanted me to do. But I was rarely, if ever, successful.

I was forced to mow the lawn, paint the house, re-roof our house, dig ditches for our irrigation system, and dig up some awful stuff in the yard called "quack grass." Since my father was employed by the public schools and received only one paycheck at the beginning of the summer, our family almost always ran out of money later in the summer. When that happened our whole family went out and picked fruit. We picked peaches, cherries, plums, pears, strawberries, and raspberries. I remember having to help significantly from age eight on. And I hated it. I cried and I screamed—literally.

I look back today and believe that my father did me an enormous amount of good by forcing me to work and work hard. I don't want to give you the impression that we never played, because we did. I remember with considerable fondness the great fun our family would have when we would finish a day's work in the summer and go to the city pool for Family Hour. And I was much older before I worked all summer long. In my younger years it was only for a two to three-week period that I worked anything approximating full time. But compared to many kids around me, and compared to almost all kids today, I was compelled to work hard.

I wasn't given any realistic choice to live a lazy life. As a consequence, my natural tendency toward laziness was eventually overcome by my father's diligence. I still have a heart that is easily tempted by laziness. But as a child I was trained up in the way I should go and now that I am old I have a very hard time departing from my training and returning to my natural state.

College, Careers, and Alternatives

As we mentioned earlier, the historical expectation was that a father was responsible for preparing his children—especially his sons—for a career. This expectation has changed—and not necessarily for the better. A subtle, but important transformation has taken place. A father's duty to provide a son with training for a career has been replaced with a father's duty to put his children through college.

There are some in the home schooling movement who say that it is always wrong for our children to attend college. I do not share this view. Unless there is a clear command in Scripture, we cannot make such a categorical pronouncement. However, providing a child with a college education merely for the sake of such an education has done little to help young people or our country.

There are some very good reasons to go to college. There are certain occupations which have legal requirements which necessitate a college education. Lawyers, doctors, teachers, and accountants are among the most notable examples of such careers.

In the days when this nation was founded, the idea of attending college was clearly tied to the purpose of training for a career. Education solely for the sake of knowledge was pursued only by sons of the very wealthy who had no thought of ever entering the working world. Even in these cases, the training of the patrician's son was done with hopes of preparing him for civic leadership. Advanced education separated from a career objective was unheard of except in rare cases involving young men who were both wealthy and lazy.

I have seen far too many young people turned into the permanent leisure class by their years in college. They go to school to learn and to party—and not necessarily in that order. A great number of very bright young people laughingly call themselves permanent students, remaining in school for eight, ten, or twelve years. Such a life is no laughing matter. Such education comes only at great expense to parents, taxpayers, or both.

A student with a four-year degree in philosophy, for example, has nothing of practical value with respect to a career unless he or she plans to go on to graduate school in order to become a philosophy professor—a very difficult task. This is not to say that students should not take philosophy courses. Such courses can be of great value in both professional and personal ways. But a student who majors in such a field has a very difficult time using the degree in any meaningful career.

We need to exercise caution about the philosophical nature of college education even when our children attend Christian colleges with a conservative reputation. The need for caution is illustrated by a recent incident.

I received same correspondence about a Christian college on the West Coast which has a reputation as a fine, theologically conservative Christian school. A dispute arose when this college cancelled a speaking engagement for a conservative congressman who is a professing Christian. This congressman has a strong reputation for opposing the gay rights movement in a very proper and effective way on Capitol Hill.

A professor from this college wrote to the president of the school complaining about the invitation. He protested the fact that this school would invite such a person with such a "negative" view of homosexuality. The professor indicated that he had learned that the militant homosexual groups Queer Nation and ACT UP were planning to protest the congressman's appearance. He said that if forced to choose, he would prefer to align himself with Queer Nation and ACT UP than with this congressman.

A student wrote a letter to the editor of the student newspaper supporting the congressman's appearance. Her position was that the students should be allowed to listen to all sides of the issue. It was obvious that she did not actually believe that the congressman's views were correct. In fact, she wrote, "There are no absolute truths in politics; even our Constitution and economic system are unjust and immoral."

This student had gone off to what her parents had undoubtedly believed was a fine Christian college. They undoubtedly expected that she would be given a thorough Christian worldview. Instead she was effectively indoctrinated in the humanistic view that there are no absolute truths. Her training in logic was equally weak. After declaring that there are no absolute truths in politics, she proceeded to declare two "truths" about our Constitution and economic system which she judged in terms of some system of absolute morality. This girl's theology, morality, and logic had been turned completely away from a scriptural understanding as a result of the instruction that she received at this "fine Christian college." We must be very alert to such problems, even with Christian colleges with the best reputations.

The traditional reason advanced for obtaining a "liberal arts" education is to expose students to a broad range of experiences to make sure that they receive the breadth of understanding necessary to relate to all of life's experiences. Let me say that I am all for a liberal arts education. But I believe that this part of a home schooled child's education should be fully completed by his or her parents before he or she leaves home.

The single most important component of a liberal arts education is accomplished by grounding children firmly in the whole counsel of the Word of God. Our children must be taught systematic doctrine and a thorough Christian worldview that has been applied to every phase of life. David Nobel's *Understanding the Times* is an excellent book to use as a resource for this purpose. Moreover, our children should be encourage to read widely in the great classics of literature. Home school students should receive from their parents the kind of training that was the educational heritage of Washington, Adams, and Madison, who were taught philosophy, logic, and classical literature.

I do not believe that college should be used as a substitute for a proper education in childhood. Build a base that is deep and wide at home and then use college primarily as preparation for a career. And if there are any legally available alternatives to college for the career path chosen for your child, then by all means seriously pursue those alternatives.

Alternatives to College

As a lawyer I endured seven years of college—four years of undergraduate school and three years of law school. During my last two years of law school I worked in a law firm thirty hours a week. I researched cases, interviewed clients, wrote simple wills, prepared witnesses for trials, and wrote briefs. During the last year of law school I even tried cases under limited circumstances as part of a legal internship program. While some of my law school classes were very good, on the whole I learned far more from working in the law office than I did by going to law school.

When I was still in law school, our firm hired a new lawyer who had gone on for an additional year of classroom instruction in tax law after graduating from law school. When it came time to go to court, he knew nothing about the process of filing papers or getting a court order signed or even withdrawing a file from the clerk's office. The firm sent me, still officially a student, to teach him the ropes.

My first day officially as a lawyer was quite different than his. Rather than simply learning how to withdraw files, I was sent by the firm on the very first Monday after I had been sworn in as a lawyer to try a weeklong real estate fraud case. They knew I had been in court dozens of times while in training and they had full confidence I could handle the case. (The jury returned a verdict for the full amount we asked for!)

My purpose in telling this story is not to tell you how wonderful I was as a young lawyer. Rather, my purpose is simply to contrast the two styles of training, apprenticeship versus classroom. Obviously, I had both. But if you were to choose only one method, apprenticeship will beat classroom instruction every time. It is a great shame that forty-eight states have laws which require attendance at law school as the only method for becoming a lawyer. Only Virginia and Washington state allow legal apprenticeship for young people to become lawyers without formal classroom instruction.

(And both of these states require a bachelor's degree as a condition of beginning legal apprenticeship.)

I am also an ordained minister. I was definitely not a professional student. I never took any form of college religion instruction. I have never attended Bible school, nor seminary, nor even a single college course in religion. But I was trained by a number of godly pastors and other Christian teachers in my life. My church believed that there was a special call of God on my life. I was engaging in a public teaching ministry, urging and equipping people to take their rightful role as Christian citizens. Accordingly, the church and denomination allowed me to apply for ordination. Our church's tradition requires the equivalent of a thesis and an oral defense much like many doctoral programs. Without any formal theological training, I wrote an extensive doctrinal statement and stood for three hours defending it before a panel of thirteen pastors. Even though the call on my life was specialized, my doctrinal statement and oral examination were on all points of doctrine traditionally covered for seminary graduates. And I passed.

I am not saying that seminary classes would not be helpful. There are many things I could learn—especially original languages, of which I know nothing. Again, my point is that there are other ways besides formal education to become prepared for a career.

I believe that apprenticeship offers far superior advantages to collegiate instruction in one very important area—the training and development of godly character.

There were no born-again Christian professors (at least that I knew of) in my law school. Outside of a limited required class on legal ethics, my professors made no attempt to teach me anything about the important questions of morality and biblical justice that are implicit in the legal profession. But Ray Eberle was there. He was my boss in the law firm and was a fine born-again man. While I learned a tremendous amount from him in terms of practical legal skills, I learned from him at least as much about practical Christian character and moral development for both personal and professional purposes.

Even though Ray Eberle gets the primary credit for training me, my father played a significant role in motivating me to become a lawyer. I can remember a conversation with my father when I was in the fourth grade. We were in the midst of a field owned by a lawyer with whom we shared irrigation water. As my dad and I walked toward the source of the irrigation system, he told me what lawyers did and also said that this was the best career to pursue if you want to be involved in political leadership. He had already instilled in me a real interest in politics. When I was in high school, he refined his "pitch." My father, a public school elementary principal, urged me to become a specialist in school law. He said that the ACLU was scaring schools to death and school districts needed sharp people to defend them from such threats.

My undergraduate honors thesis was written on school law. I took a number of education courses to make sure I knew something substantive about the topic as well. Neither my dad nor I ever dreamed I would become a lawyer who was constantly in court battling against school districts. But when we talked and planned in the 1950s and 1960s we never dreamed that secular humanism, New Age curriculum, or condoms would be the subjects of instruction in the public schools either.

My father gave me a career vision from the earliest ages. As best I can remember, he talked with me about a number of things, but the real encouragement from him came when a career path he mentioned seemed to strike a real responsive chord with me.

Let's synthesize a few basic principles:

1. Fathers need to supply the motivation for a successful career.

It doesn't matter if your child is interested in auto mechanics or brain surgery, the motivation to succeed is a necessary ingredient for every child. Fathers have a special obligation to inspire a desire for excellence and success (measured in Christian terms) in each of their children.

2. College is not a substitute for career preparation.

Dads, don't hide behind your checkbook and say, "I paid $50,000 for a college education, the rest is up to him." College educations are expensive. The same amount of money could provide a start in a small business. If your child pursues a career path that includes or requires college, fine. But don't throw away either your money or your child's future and buy the sales pitch of those who want to sell you $50,000 worth of English literature. Remember, it is a business transaction (at least in part) from their side of the equation. If education is solely for altruistic purposes, why do parents or taxpayers have to pay for it?

These same cautions are true of Christian colleges. Teach your children philosophy and a Christian worldview at home. If you want your children to have supplemental, specialized training in developing a Christian worldview, send them to the two-week program offered by Summit Ministries in Manitou Springs, Colorado. If you want them to spend some time getting well rounded and enlarging their frame of reference, send them on a short-term missions project to another culture.

This may sound totally anti-college. I do not mean to convey such a message. There are good reasons to go to college. Not every course at college needs to be directly related to a career subject. It is often appropriate to take classes in English literature (lest my earlier example be misunderstood). I am simply urging that the majority of the time and expense of college should be spent for career preparation, not personal enrichment.

3. Pursue apprenticeship opportunities whenever possible.

There is no legitimate reason why the vast majority of pastors cannot obtain necessary preparation through apprenticeship. Young men can train under one or more pastors and learn every subject taught in seminary, including original languages. At the same time they can learn practical character development from a godly role model.

There are many other careers that can be presently obtained through apprenticeship. Home schoolers need to do what we can to expand and encourage this avenue of training.

However, we need to speak honestly about the subject of professional apprenticeship under current circumstances. If you have a child who wants to become a doctor, dentist, lawyer, architect, or a member of any other profession licensed by the government, your child is not going to be able to obtain the necessary license without a formal education.

Many home schoolers have a strong vision for apprenticeship. Unfortunately, a number of home schooling families misunderstand current realities. Currently your children cannot become a doctor, a lawyer, or any other licensed professional purely through the apprenticeship model. There is no question that your children can learn many important things about these professions through apprenticeship alone. But there is a world of difference between being knowledgeable about law and being a lawyer. We need to try to push back the barriers by taking maximum advantage of the limited opportunities available for apprenticeship. But we do our children and ourselves a disservice if we hold out a promise of a career which cannot be achieved solely through apprenticeship. We should work to make the apprenticeship model legally acceptable for every profession.

4. Don't forget your daughters.

I have six girls and very traditional Christian views about the role of women in the church and home. Nonetheless, I feel an obligation to prepare my daughters for careers in the same way the Proverbs 31 women was prepared for a career of retail marketing and real estate transactions.

Women may be called to singleness. If so, they need to have proper preparation for a career which will earn them a proper living.

As my older daughters approach their mid to late teens, my current thinking is to encourage them to pursue training that has the dual purpose of helping them as wives and (home schooling) mothers, as well as serving as a back up career should the need arise.

For example, my oldest daughter loves piano and is seriously considering college-level training in music and piano. This is obviously an area which can be used for ministry at church and home and which also has the potential of being used as a career (piano teacher, etc.) should the need arise.

I want my daughters to have business savvy like the woman honored in Proverbs 31. But I don't want them chasing the feminist dream of the two-career marriage (or shall we say "living arrangement"). They can't have it all, as many feminists are beginning to find out. I want to avoid the twin evils of neglecting the proper career training of my daughters, on the one hand, and pushing them to the feminist career mold, on the other. Proverbs 31 teaches a godly balance: A woman who possesses work skills and financial resources, but who uses those skills in a way that keeps her home with her children and husband. The woman in Proverbs 31 does not stay home barefoot and pregnant watching soap operas. She is busy with more than garden clubs and poetry societies. Yet, she is first and foremost at home with her children and husband.

In fact, home schooling offers women the best of both worlds. Home schooling is a job that society values—teaching academics to children. It provides serious intellectual stimulation. It provides many opportunities to be held in esteem by people outside your family. My wife is regularly treated as a superwoman by Christians and non-Christians alike when they find out she home schools eight children. The pay is low. But the ability to be home with your children while working is second to none.

My wife was a very good student in high school and college. Before we began home schooling she would sometimes complain about the lack of intellectual activity in her life of wiping spills, changing diapers, and doing laundry. A couple of times she even wondered out loud about the idea of going to work.

Since we have been home schooling, her need for intellectual challenge has been abundantly satisfied. She has always believed that a mother's place is in the home. But home schooling turned this belief into an intellectually satisfying lifestyle which provides many tangible rewards. The career I will "push" at my daughters is the same one practiced by their mother.

Train your children to work hard and take initiative when they are young. Give them a broad liberal arts education while they are being home schooled. Then help them focus on a career path that will provide them with a real world living as well as make use of their spiritual gifts.

Chapter 5

Preparing Your Child for Marriage

I have gone parasailing, skied down black diamond slopes, tried to waterski barefoot, met with Soviet Christians who were being trailed by the KGB, and gone on the Phil Donahue Show—twice. But far and away the most dangerous activity I ever tried was dating.

Although I became a Christian when I was six, I did not follow God's standards for dating in my teenage years. While I can truthfully say that I did not know God's complete standards in this area, I have to admit that I did not follow the light I did have. Even though I was a "good kid" by the world's standards, I dated non-Christian girls and engaged in other practices that the world finds harmless but which violate God's principles.

Not only was my dating pattern in violation of Scripture, but when my wife and I got married we also made some significant mistakes as judged by God's standards. (For example, we got married much earlier than her parents wanted.) Even though things have worked out for us, we know all too well that we have had to pay a great price in our lives for our failures in this area. We have had to spend countless hours working on our marriage to correct the mistakes we made during dating and our mistaken actions surrounding our marriage. I will recount a few of these mistakes throughout this chapter to illustrate certain points.

For right now, suffice it to say that my wife and I were not ready for marriage when we got married. We were lacking in both major areas we will discuss in this chapter—practical preparation and spiritual preparation

We now have two teenaged daughters—one is in her late teens. They are clearly and objectively attractive girls. But neither has ever been on a date. And as far as we are all concerned—girls and parents alike—there is no likelihood that there will be any dates in the near future.

Vickie and I are of the opinion that we have not invested more than a decade in home schooling attempting to raise godly children just to have all this hard work thrown away by allowing our girls to marry some unprepared spiritual midget.

Our older daughters (we haven't really discussed this with our two-year-old) have committed themselves to the idea that they will pursue a relationship with a boy only when it is consistent with these three principles:

1. Both the young man and I are prepared for marriage.
2. I am investigating this particular young man because he appears to meet the spiritual standards my parents and I have agreed upon for a husband.
3. I find him to be personally interesting and attractive.

The vast majority of people engage in dating based solely on the third criteria. I know I did.

In home schooling circles there is a lot of talk about courtship versus dating. The major difference between courtship and dating is discovered by simply following all three of the above-listed criteria rather than engaging in dating based solely on personal attraction and interest.

Get an Early Commitment to Courtship

Dads, your first job in this area is to secure your children's commitment to following all three of the above principals in relations with the opposite sex. Don't wait until they are sixteen or seventeen. You will have waited far too long. I can't remember for sure how young our children were when we first began discussing these matters. But I know that by the time our oldest daughter was ten or eleven years old, serious discussions were underway.

In fact, it is never too early to start teaching your children a different standard from the world. When I was growing up, it was expected from the earliest ages that every boy would have a girlfriend. I can remember the name of my "girlfriends" in second grade, third grade, and fourth grade. Three different girls. This set a pattern for many years of my life. The cultural expectation was that all of us would be pairing off into romantic relationships more than a decade and a half before any of us could legitimately think of marriage.

These early relationships were not harmless. Not only did they set bad patterns, but also encouraged emotional commitments that seemed to pop up from time to time for a number of years.

By the time I was in junior high, some of my friends were engaging in sexual intercourse. After all, they had been "going with girls" for years and were tired of waiting for "the real thing." I was much more innocent in this area than some. But I was not totally unscathed. I kissed a great number of girls. And for this pattern of behavior I paid a great spiritual price.

Vickie and I have raised our children with different expectations. Any discussion of boy-girl relationships is always in the context of a possible marriage partner. As a consequence, even our beautiful, blond seventeen-year-old daughter has never had a boyfriend. And she has no regrets about this. Obviously, we are thrilled.

The same things are true of our fifteen-year-old and our twelve-year-old. Many of the girls their age are already seriously into dating and more.

Let me restate this preventative principle: From the very earliest ages, raise your children with the understanding that the whole area of boy-girl relationships is to be reserved for the time of life just prior to marriage. I know for a fact that I was indoctrinated into the "religion" of secular humanism through public school and secular college education. But the damage done to me by that indoctrination was less severe and easier to correct than the damage done by the societal philosophy of early dating.

The vast majority of parents want their children to abstain from sexual relationships until marriage. However, we have failed to see that abstinence should include emotional abstinence as well. In other words, if we permit our children to develop boyfriend-girlfriend relationships before they are ready to get married, we are simply asking for sexual temptation, and in many cases, sexual trouble.

Through my teens I was involved in a number of emotional relationships. And these emotional attachments created a certain level of physical involvement. I drew a line which kept me from total physical involvement, yet in my spirit 1 knew that I was violating God's standards of purity. And I used to think that my failure was to draw a more righteous physical line. But I now understand that I should have drawn the line at the level of any emotional involvement with a girlfriend before I was ready to start seriously looking for a wife. Crossing that emotional line made it virtually impossible to stay on the right side of the physical line.

The pressures of society today no longer affirm sexual restraint; rather, these pressures push children toward full sexual intimacy. We ask too much of our kids to restrain their physical involvement while they engaged in emotional romance.

Home schoolers who protect their children from secular humanism, but fail to protect their children from even greater damage, which can arise from premature boy-girl relationships, are missing a critical opportunity to raise godly children.

Fathers, it is up to you to set the standards for your family. You can ensure that your children escape the dangerous trap of premature emotional and physical romance. Train them up with the home-based culture and expectation that romantic love (boy-girl relationships) is reserved for the time of life just before marriage.

Let's now turn to the three principles of courtship and how, as fathers, we can work to ensure that our children are really ready for marriage.

Courtship Principle No. 1

Courtship Should Wait Until One is Prepared for Marriage.

Your sons have at least three practical areas in which they need to be prepared for marriage: career and finances, home maintenance, and fatherhood.

Your daughters have at least three areas in which they need practical preparation as well: teaching, homemaking, and motherhood.

Preparing Your Sons for Marriage

1. A man is not ready for marriage until he is ready to work and take care of his family's finances.

Scripture makes it clear that a man should be embarked upon his career before he begins to build his family.

> *Finish your outdoor work and get your fields ready; after that, build your house.*
>
> Prov. 24:27

> *If anyone does not provide for his relatives, and especially for his immediate family, he has denied the faith and is worse than an unbeliever.*
>
> 1 Tim. 5:8

Men who are not ready to work are not ready for marriage. When I say this, I say it to my own shame.

My wife and I were married just before our junior year in college. I knew prior to marriage that I wanted to be a lawyer. Accordingly, I knew that I was facing five more years of college before I could begin working full time.

Our plan was for both of us to finish undergraduate school. Vickie's parents were prepared to pay for her college expenses, while I supported myself with loans and part-time jobs—supplemented with help from my parents. Then our plan was that I would enter a prestigious law school as a day student while my wife would teach full time to support our family.

I am not saying that it was unpleasant to be married during college and law school. It was very, very pleasant and good for me in many ways. My college grades went from just under a 3.0 average to nearly a 4.0 average. It was one of the best times in our lives. But it was irresponsible for me to get married before the time I was ready to care for a family.

Our plan for my wife to teach and support our family never materialized. She was able to only get substitute teaching work for one year and got pregnant during my second year of law school. And at that point we decided that her days of working outside the home were over.

The idea of attending a prestigious law school didn't work out either. I ended up going to an evening division of an average law school. I took one class during the day so I could finish in three years. During my second and third years of law school I worked as a legal intern for a Christian lawyer. I earned enough at this job to pay basic living expenses for our family. However, I did not earn enough to pay for law school. Accordingly, we had to rely on student loans and help from our families to make it through.

It was a very hard financial struggle. And God used these struggles for our good. For one thing, it has made me much more sensitive to people in need than I might have been otherwise. But the biggest lesson I learned is that the way I went through school is man's way of doing things, not God's way.

It is clear to me now that a man is not ready for marriage until he is ready to care for his family. It is a real danger for a man to get married when he is still in the season of preparing for work. Many of my friends in law school who went through school while married ended up in divorce shortly after the conclusion of law school.

I would be hesitant to say that a man should never be married while going to college or graduate school. But this should be the exception rather than the rule. If you go to the average seminary, most men are married. Consequently, there is enormous financial pressure on these families—including pressure on wives to go to work.

Unless a person has the funds from work, savings, or an inheritance to support his family while attending further training, then I think there should be a presumption that such training is not God's will for a married man. This presumption can be overcome by clear leading from God. But I think that we should remember Hudson Taylor's rule to determine God's direction in life: What God orders He pays for.

Daughters and careers.

Let's briefly discuss career preparation for daughters. If it sounds a bit old fashioned to emphasize a man's duty to provide for his family, then so be it. This book is intended to paint an idealistic picture, and from a scriptural standpoint, there is no question that the ideal situation is where the mother is free to stay home with her children.

I recognize that not all women will get married. Nor will all married women be able to have babies. And some women will end up in divorce or will be widowed. So it is necessary for a woman to give some serious consideration about a career as well. Accordingly, Vickie and I plan to have each of our daughters do some planning and preparation for a career.

But my context here is *preparation for marriage*. Within this context, I believe it is unnecessary to have a woman prepared for a career outside the home as a prerequisite to marriage.

Financial management.

A man's ability to provide for his family's needs means more than simply having a career. It means that he is able to provide for and manage the financial needs for his household. This means that a husband needs to know how to balance a checkbook, make a budget, and do short- and long-range financial planning.

Your children, but especially your sons, need to be schooled in the biblical principles of finances. I would strongly encourage you to teach your children these princi-ples by using *Surviving the Money Jungle* (junior high age) or *Getting a Grip on Your Money* (high school age and up) by Larry Burkett or by using some other good Christian mate-rial on finances. (These books are available through Money Matters, P.O. Box 100, Gainesville, GA 30503.)

Your children, and especially your sons, should be given basic training in dealing with health insurance, and under-standing life insurance, pension plans, and savings.

In short, your son should be ready to deal with the adult financial world as a fully schooled person before he should be considered ready for marriage.

2. A man is not ready for marriage until he is able to maintain a home.

Let me confess that I absolutely hate home maintenance projects. I am not a handyman in the slightest. But unless a person is wealthy enough to employ a full-time handyman, it is a fact of life that men need to be able to maintain a home. Faucets need to be fixed, lawns need to be mowed, and cars need to be maintained.

To some degree, it is good to teach daughters these things. But I am old fashioned enough to believe that men should bear the primary responsibility in this area.

My father used to take me down to a self-service garage where he taught me how to change the oil and lubricate the car. I had absolutely no aptitude in this area, but I did it anyway. In my late teens I was given the bulk of the task of re-roofing our home. And a year or so later I had a substantial part of the responsibility for painting the exterior of our house.

It was good for me to do these things. And when my oldest son gets a little older (he's four now), I will begin the process of teaching him the few skills I have.

Our older daughters have learned some home maintenance skills. But again, I believe that a more intensive training will be necessary for our sons. It will probably be necessary to have them go down the street to the home of a grandfather from our church to learn some skills I am unable to teach them. But it is my responsibility to make sure that my sons get the necessary opportunity to learn some minimum level of home maintenance skills.

3. A man is not ready for marriage until he is prepared to be a father.

Since this whole book is dedicated to a discussion of fatherhood, it would be unnecessarily repetitive to detail the attributes of fatherhood. At this point, suffice it to say that older sons need to be taught (at a minimum) the full content of our discussions in this book.

Another thing that deserves emphasis is this: Marriage and fatherhood go hand in hand. Our culture has done its best to paint a picture of married life that separates sex from the possibility of becoming a parent.

As biblical Christians, we need to understand that it is still true today that "children are a reward from the Lord" (Ps. 127:3 paraphrase). A man who gets married with the understanding that "we won't have children for a few years" is not ready to get married. Even for those willing to use birth control, children may come along due to the Lord's sovereignty despite man's best efforts to the contrary. If a man marries unprepared for fatherhood, there is a possibility that he will become an unprepared father.

Prepare your son to be a first-rate spiritual leader for your grandchildren. Obviously, he will learn far more by observing you than from merely listening to you. Do a good job day in and day out and your son will have a great foundation for his own family.

Preparing Your Daughters for Marriage

Let's consider three areas of special concern for the practical preparation of our daughters for marriage: teaching, homemaking, and motherhood.

1. A daughter should be prepared to teach her children.

I believe in home schooling. I will not consider my home schooling a success until I see my daughters and sons home schooling their own children. Accordingly, I have a special concern that my daughters be prepared to teach their own children when the time comes.

I am not suggesting that we are going to send our girls into specialized training in educational psychology or classroom methodology. Much of this type of training is counterproductive in the home schooling context. Much of it is philosophically unacceptable to biblical Christians.

It is true that moms who do not have a solid academic preparation can work hard and do an excellent job of home schooling. Nonetheless, a solid academic background is an asset for a home schooling mom. This is one additional reason why we should strive for excellence in home schooling.

Your daughters (and sons too) should be encouraged to help with the teaching of younger brothers and sisters. Our girls have done this to some degree. They are also engaged in teaching Sunday school for younger children.

Learning to work with younger children plus a solid academic background is worth far more than college courses in educational methodology

2. A daughter should be prepared to be a homemaker.

My wife is now an excellent cook. But she had only the most minimal experience in cooking prior to our marriage. She did very, very well academically. But she devoted virtually all her time to academics and very little time to practical preparation for keeping a home.

As measured by achievement test scores, our older daughters are performing on approximately the same level of academics that my wife and I attained in high school. But our daughters can run circles around either of us in terms of their ability to manage a home.

The older two girls can cook just about anything. Katie, our twelve-year-old, is on the way to this same level of attainment. They know from long experience how to clean bathrooms, vacuum, wash dishes, do wash, etc, etc.

While mothers will be doing the vast majority of training in homemaking, dads need to serve as encouragers and undertake some of the training as well.

Some moms are so committed to perfectionism that they will tend to do everything themselves so they know it will get done correctly. Other moms will feel guilty if they have their children doing a lot of work around the house. Dads, you need to encourage your wife to see the opportunities for training. And Dads, you shouldn't complain if things aren't perfect. Some moms act like perfectionists because their husbands demand it. If you are this kind of dad, ease off a little and let the kids learn by doing.

3. A daughter should be prepared to be a mother.

Girls need to be taught how to care for newborns. They should learn to be able to deal with children in each of the stages of a child's life. They should learn patience, love, and devotion. All of these things are ideally taught by observing their mothers with their younger brothers and sisters. When we finally get to the end of the line and our youngest children are in their teens, Vickie and I expect that our children will learn practical child-rearing skills by helping in the homes of their older brothers and sisters.

If you have no younger children for your teens to work with, there are opportunities for interacting with younger children somewhere in your church or home schooling support group. Avail yourselves of opportunities to train your older children while providing some needed support for home schooling families with younger children as well.

Courtship Principle No. 2

I Will Not Consider Any Person for Courtship Unless He Or She Meets The Spiritual Standards I Have Established Together with My Parents.

My oldest daughter (with the help of her mother and sister) has compiled a "little" list of qualities that she will look for in a husband.

Character Qualities for My Future Husband
by Christy Farris

1. He must be a born-again Christian, able to give testimony of his salvation.
2. He should be patient.
3. He should be kind.
4. He should not be envious.

5. He should be humble.
6. He should be not easily angered.
7. He should not hold a grudge.
8. He should not delight in evil.
9. He should rejoice with the truth.
10. He must be a protector.
11. He should be trusting.
12. He should have hope.
13. He must persevere.
14. He should be loving.
15. He should be joyful.
16. He should be good.
17. He should be peaceful.
18. He should be faithful.
19. He should be gentle.
20. He must have self-control.
21. He must be a hard worker.
22. He must love the Lord with all his heart, soul, mind, and body.
23. He should walk in all God's ways.
24. He must hold fast to the Lord.
25. He should not worry, but turn to God in prayer.
26. He should press onward toward the goal.
27. He should build others up with his words.
28. He must have not even a hint of sexual immorality or impurity.
29. He must not joke coarsely or say inappropriate things.

30. He must not be greedy.
31. He must not be yoked with unbelievers.
32. He should be the salt of the earth and the light of the world and obey the Great Commission.
33. He must like children.
34. He must be committed to attending church regularly.
35. He should keep his priorities straight.
36. He must have a sense of humor.
37. Mom and Dad must like him and approve of him.
38. He should not be overweight (a violation of the principle of self-control).
39. He must be prepared to support a family.
40. He must he prepared to be the spiritual leader of the home.
41. He must be committed to staying out of debt.
42. He must want to home school our children.
43. He should have some kind of musical ability.
44. He must be attractive to me.
45. He must have daily quiet times with the Lord.

The problem with her list is that only one man ever lived a perfect life. And she knows that it will be impossible to find a young man possessing all of these qualities in full measure. (Please note that some qualities are listed as "musts." From these qualities there can be no deviation.) But when she looks at a young man with these kinds of qualities in mind, she will be a lot better off than if she simply was looking for a guy who "is cute and makes me laugh." The key thing is mastery of the fundamental qualities and a teachable spirit.

Once she has found a young man appearing to have a food start on this list, then the period of courtship should be long enough to know that the young man will continue to make progress toward these areas of spiritual maturity.

Many of the character qualities on my daughter's list are obviously taken from the characteristics of love set forth in 1 Corinthians 13 and from the fruits of the Spirit in Galatians 5:22-23. These qualities certainly apply with equal force to the evaluation of a young woman as a suitable wife. Many of the others listed are only applicable to a man. A few (musical ability, for example) are simply my daughter's personal preferences.

My purpose in sharing this list is not to have you adopt it line for line for your own children, but rather to give you a starting point in working with your children to create lists of their own.

Here are some additional qualities to look for in a young woman, taken from Proverbs 31. I didn't check to see if they are all accurately represented, should I?

1. She should have noble character.
2. She should be worthy of her husband's confidence.
3. She should be working toward her husband's good, not his harm.

4. She should be willing to work eagerly with her hands (i.e., willing to do practical tasks).
5. She should be willing to sacrifice her own comfort for the needs of her family (i.e., willing to get up early to feed her family).
6. She should be financially resourceful.
7. She should be diligent.
8. She should be willing to love and serve the poor.
9. She should plan ahead for the needs of her family.
10. She should take good care of herself to keep herself attractive to her husband (v.22). Why list this one separately?
11. She should inspire and encourage her husband to be a leader in the community.
12. She should be strong and dignified.

Let me add one more thing. A commitment to look for people possessing these spiritual qualities means a commitment to raising our children to possess these qualities as well. We should not expect our children to attract spiritual champions unless they are of championship quality themselves.

Courtship Principle No. 3

I Will Only Court a Person Whom I Find Personally Interesting and Attractive.

It will be really easy to get your kids to agree with this principle. And it seems so obvious as to not merit discussion.

However, I have observed some instances in home schooling circles and on the part of other Christians to view any consideration of physical attraction to be unspiritual. Let me say that I would not want to be married to a woman that I found uninteresting or unattractive. I cannot read the Song of Solomon without believing that God intended for us to find pleasure in our spouses.

The problem is that the world uses physical attraction and an interesting personality as the exclusive criteria for marriage. We should not overreact to the world's excesses by totally devaluing this consideration.

If our kids marry someone solely out of spiritual altruism, they will face special temptations from the world's way of thinking. And someday, they may find another person who appears to possess many good qualities and for whom they have a special chemistry or attraction. That will be a very dangerous situation.

This does not mean that we should allow ourselves to develop a mindset that we keep looking for a more attractive partner. On the contrary, it is serial dating which endorses and creates this way of thinking. But to ignore physical attractiveness altogether is foolish.

Actually more important than physical attractiveness is the ability to find the other person interesting. Friendship is a very important component of a good marriage. Our children should be encouraged to place considerable value on pursuing courtship with a proven friend.

A couple who can dream big dreams together has a bond of a common vision that is priceless. Teach your kids to get beneath the surface and find a person who has dreams and plans for life which are compatible with and complementary to their own.

God wants the best for us. He wants us to have enjoyable, exciting marriages. Our kids don't have to marry duds just because we value spiritual qualities. The principle of keeping things in balance has no more important application than in courtship and choosing a marriage partner.

Dads, there are no more crucial steps you can take to ensure the spiritual vitality of your descendants than to help your children break out of the world's grip and choose life partners based on the principles of the Word of God.

Chapter 6

Preparing Your Child for Citizenship

*H*ome schoolers have an opportunity to influence our country for good. First of all, by our own actions and commitments we can help move society in the direction of moral and fiscal sanity. But I believe we can have an even greater impact as we raise up a generation of children with the knowledge, skills, and vision necessary to influence and lead our nation.

As I mentioned briefly in earlier chapters, my father had a profound impact in motivating me toward a career in law and politics. He told me stories of the deep-seated corruption he had witnessed in his home county in Arkansas. This gave me knowledge of the "real world" and it placed a burning desire in my soul to fight against wrongdoing. He explained the evils of communism to me and taught me principles of religious liberty, free enterprise, and individualism. When I was nine or ten years old he explained the details of how an outsider was elected to the local school board by some very clever political moves. This gave me an appreciation of the importance of mastering the procedural aspects of politics. He took me to school board meetings where I saw a display of the skills of public speaking and backroom politics. He always voted (as did my mother) and always discussed the reasons for voting. And though he almost always voted Republican, time and again he would say, "Choose the man, not the party."

My father did not set out to deliberately make me into a political aficionado. He was simply interested in government and he took the time to tell his son about it in the regular course of living.

Some fathers have a natural interest in politics; others do not. Regardless of whether you have a natural interest or not, it is your duty as a father to ensure that your children are given systematic training in citizenship.

Let me suggest eight principles we should teach our children in order to ensure that they have the necessary foundation to become good citizens. In the course of enumerating these principles, I will suggest some projects designed to reinforce these principles.

Let me say that this list is not exhaustive by any stretch of the imagination. The principles listed are the ones which occur to me to be the most important, but you may have other or differing ideas which you should implement.

My book, *Where Do I Draw The Line?*, published by Bethany House, is exclusively devoted to giving advice for practical citizenship skills for Christians. This book may be a good resource for you.

I am fully convinced of the importance of teaching children the principles of freedom. If our children do not believe in freedom, they will not remain free for very long.

Eight Principles of Freedom

1. The Bible speaks to every area of life, including our responsibility as citizens.

Proverbs 3:6 says, "in all your ways acknowledge Him, and He will make your paths straight." (See also Matthew 5:13 which commands us to be salt of the earth.) Being salt of the earth means that we are to act as a preserving agent in our society. Ephesians 5:11 commands us to "Have nothing to do with the fruitless deeds of darkness, but rather expose them." In Psalm 94:16 God asks, "Who will rise up for me against the wicked? Who will take a stand for me against evildoers?"

When I was growing up, the prevailing attitude in my home church was that politics and Christianity were to be kept as far apart as the east is from the west. My father was a new Christian, and thus didn't argue with the leaders taking this view, but at home he taught me differently.

Eventually, the Christian community woke up. We now understand that our duty as Christians does extend to every area of life—including our responsibilities as citizens. We need to learn to analyze political issues from Biblical perspectives.

Here are some suggested projects to teach your children that the Bible speaks to politics just as to every other area of life:

- Study Deuteronomy 17:14-20. Hundreds of years before the people clamored for a king, God told Israel the proper standard for picking a political leader. As a family, analyze the various attributes kings were supposed to have. Restate these attributes in modern terms. Discuss the president, your governor, mayor, congressman, and other leaders in light of these attributes. Look at Hosea 8 (especially v.4) and determine the consequences of picking leaders who do not have God's approval.

- Read one chapter from the book of Proverbs each day for a month as a family. Ask your children to identify both good and bad examples of how political, media, and entertainment figures illustrate the principles in Proverbs.

2. Our nation should be governed by the higher law principles set forth in the Declaration of Independence and the Constitution of the United States.

Because of my great love for the Constitution and my concern for the training of the next generation in citizenship principles, I have written a high-school-level (or higher) textbook entitled *Constitutional Law for Christian Students* (available through HSLDA). I liked the book very much when I wrote it. After I taught it to my two high school daughters I loved it. Let me very briefly synthesize one of the most important principles taught at length in this book.

There is an old saying, "Ours is a government of laws, not men." What this means is that the people who govern our nation are not above the law, but are subject to it themselves. Presidents are not kings who can issue whatever decree suits them, but must take only the actions authorized by the law.

Because of the principle of higher law embodied in our Constitution, leaders cannot pass any law they want. They can pass only such laws as are authorized by the Constitution. The Constitution limits the power of the officials.

While it is true that men can change the Constitution, it is an extraordinarily difficult thing to do. Mere majorities can never change the Constitution.

America created the idea of government limited by a constitution. It was premised on our understanding of God's Word. This is a law that is higher than man and which man cannot change. Leaders are subject to God's laws. Therefore, they can be subjected to man-made higher law as well.

- Read the Declaration of Independence as a family. What is the official name of this document? Who do you think was the intended audience(s) for reading the Declaration? Did you know that the Continental Congress actually voted on July 2, 1776, to separate from England? What were we saying differently here on July 4, 1776? (All the answers to these questions [if you need them] are contained in chapter 2 of *Constitutional Law for Christian Students.*)

- Discuss the account of Richard Nixon being driven from office because of the Watergate scandal. How does this illustrate the principle of higher law?

- Read the Bill of Rights. List all the limitations you can find on the power of the federal government. Where are people directly granted any rights? (Hint: most amendments contain no grants of rights; they contain only limitations on government power.) The only way to give people rights is to limit government power.

3. The individual, the family, the church, and the government are all given differing spheres of jurisdiction. Each should responsibly and faithfully exercise the duties within its own jurisdiction and not infringe on the prerogatives of the other.

The fundamental problem with government at this stage of our nation's history is that those running the government have no understanding of the proper purposes for government. Most people running for Congress make promises which seem to imply that they intend to pass federal legislation to solve every problem in life. Families have a need for baby-sitters while moms leave their children to go off and work. So Congress recently passed a law using federal tax dollars to pay for a massive baby-sitting program. Baby-sitting has become a federal issue thanks to a do-it-all, spend-it-all Congress.

As compassionate as it seems, it violates a fundamental principle of personal responsibility for the federal government to pay to rebuild homes and businesses after a natural disaster. Why should your family be required to pay additional taxes because I did not exercise personal responsibility and buy insurance for my home or business? The government should help in such situations, but that help should be limited and not serve as a substitute for personal responsibility.

A current political issue in my home state of Virginia absolutely defies logic. The governor, Doug Wilder, wants the taxpayers of Virginia to pay for a new football stadium so that Jack Kent Cooke, an elderly billionaire, can make more money by selling more tickets than in the current stadium.

There was a season of American history where elderly billionaires went around the country constructing buildings and giving them to the public—Carnegie Libraries, for example. Why is it the responsibility of government to help a billionaire make more money? We have totally lost the sense that government has limited purposes and limited duties.

The Bible teaches individual responsibility. I am responsible to take care of myself. "If a man will not work, he shall not eat" (2 Thess. 3:10). The Bible teaches that men should take care of their families. "If anyone does not provide for his relatives, and especially for his immediate family, he has denied the faith and is worse than an unbeliever" (1 Tim. 5:8). The Bible teaches that parents are responsible for the education of their children. (See, for example, Deuteronomy 4:10, 31:13; Isaiah 38:19; Ephesians 6:4.)

The Bible teaches that churches are to take care of the widows within their midst who have no family to care for them (1 Tim. 5). The Bible teaches that we are to assist our brothers and sisters in need (Acts 2:45 paraphrase). The Bible teaches, in the parable of the good Samaritan, that we should tenderly care for even strangers who we come upon in dire or emergent need (Luke 10:25-37).

The history of Christian humanitarian projects is a worthy testimony to efforts to fulfill these duties of the church.

The Bible teaches that government is to administer justice (Rom. 13:3 general context). Government is to provide defense for its people (Luke 14:31 general context). Government is intended to "punish those who do wrong and to commend those who do right" (1 Pet. 2:14).

Our nation would be better off if families, churches, and the government each did a good job of executing its own duties and left the duties of the others alone.

We need to wrestle with the problems that arise when one of these institutions fails to carry out its duties. For example, what happens if a father doesn't care for his own? The government has to take care of those children, doesn't it?

Not necessarily. There are many things government can and should do in the case of a father who is capable of caring for his own but who simply refuses. (The most frequent modern example of this is a refusal to pay child support.)

In such a case, the government should punish the defaulting father because he is doing wrong. The state of Wisconsin recently instituted a program where fathers who refused to pay child support and claimed they could not find jobs were forced to go to work part time for free doing community service projects like picking up trash along the highways. A huge percentage of these fathers were suddenly able to find work.

Substantially less government welfare would be called for if we simply required both immediate and extended families to take care of their own.

Another aspect of this same problem is that government refuses to even recognize jurisdictional limitations on the varying levels of government.

I once walked from the federal courthouse in Albany, New York, to the office of the New York State Department of Education. On my journey between these two huge buildings, I passed other large buildings housing city government and county government offices as well.

Seeing all those buildings in one walk graphically reminded me that Americans are burdened with too many levels of government. As I passed this series of buildings, I literally said out loud, "The poor taxpayers of New York." Every level of government seems to believe that it has sweeping responsibilities and very few limitations.

Every place in this country has at least three "departments of education" (federal, state, and local) supervising the public schools. Some places have four levels of educational bureaucracy. Why do we need local school districts, supervised by county educational agencies, supervised by state departments of education, and meddled with by the federal department of education? Taxpayers are being required to pay for the salaries of tens of thousands of educational bureaucrats who never teach a child, all because the various levels of government don't seem to understand their unique purposes.

Our country needs to go through a process of deciding which level of government is responsible for each function of government—education, building roads, providing police and fire protection, etc. We must eliminate virtually all duplications of services.

Each level of government needs to know its mission and do it well. And it needs to stay out of the jurisdiction of other levels of government.

- Find a person who has a need that the government would normally try to meet. Have your family help to meet that need in lieu of government assistance.

- Have your child write to an education official at the local, state, and federal department of education. Ask them to explain why we need so many layers of educational bureaucracy and if the money wouldn't be better spent by investing in teachers and textbooks rather than extra layers of bureaucrats. Discuss the answers you get.

- Send a similar letter to your congressman, governor, state legislator, county board of supervisors (or its equivalent), and a school board member. Discuss the answers you get from each.

- Discuss how you will handle the situation when members in your family get older and need special care.

4. *Every person should have an equal opportunity, not an equal result.*

Many people today believe that everyone has a right to a successful life. There is a big difference between the right to try to succeed and the right to succeed. Freedom requires the freedom to fail as well as the freedom to succeed.

America is a nation committed to fundamental fairness. We want the referees in a football game to call the game with equal justice to both sides. We believe that home teams should have no special advantage.

Our political and legal system should operate with this principle of fundamental fairness. All people should have equal treatment before the law as individuals.

While the government should be required to treat every individual equally, how does this principle apply to private persons and businesses?

There is a general rule of freedom that protects private transactions. A business owner can hire only Harvard graduates if he wants and can refuse to hire someone for the sole reason that he or she graduated from Yale. A landlady renting her basement apartment can make a rule that she will not rent to anyone who smokes. If she wanted to, she could also refuse to rent to anyone unless he or she smoked. Freedom requires us to allow people to arrange their private lives any way they want even if it appears to be foolish to us.

However, we have decided as a nation that there are some concepts that are so important that we are willing to forfeit a part of our freedom to accomplish these other goals. Racial equality is the principal example of one such principle. We are so committed to racial equality that we willingly override the general rules of freedom to make sure that no person may receive different treatment because of the color of his or her skin.

We have the same commitment to the principle of religious toleration. Except in employment opportunities directly related to a religious organization, our commitment to religious equality overrides the general principle of freedom, and accordingly, religious discrimination in employment is banned.

There are very few principles that are so important that they are worth overriding our general rule of freedom. The whole idea of so-called gay rights laws is that homosexuals are asking the rest of society to give up our freedom to advance their "lifestyle." In order to favor a gay rights law a person must determine that the advancement of homosexuality is more important than our general commitment to freedom. I, for one, do not believe that immoral (and in many states illegal) behavior should ever be the basis for requiring a forfeiture of our general principle of freedom.

- Discuss the results of the economic system in the Soviet Union that guaranteed equal results for all people.

- Read a history of Jamestown and discuss the results of the settlers' efforts to guarantee equality of result.

- An older child can do a research paper on all of the utopian movements in this country, which have attempted to guarantee an equal economic result to all.

- Institute a plan (for a short period) that everyone gets to eat regardless of whether he or she does his or her chores. Then have a plan where people get to eat only if they do their chores. Have your children compare the cleanliness of your house under these two different plans.

5. As good stewards of the freedom we have been given, Christians have a duty to exercise their responsibilities as citizens.

I give a lengthy defense of the proposition that Christians have a biblical duty to be involved in the public affairs of our nation in my book *Where Do I Draw The Line?* For now, I simply point to three passages in Scripture.

Matthew 5:13 says that we are to be the salt of the earth. Salt, in biblical times, was primarily used as a preservative. The salt of the earth is intended to be a moral preservative in the society in which we live. This means that we have to effectively take a stand against sin. Since so much sin today is officially sanctioned by government (abortion, pornography, etc.), effective opposition to sin requires our involvement in the affairs of our government.

Ephesians 5: 11 says, "Have nothing to do with the fruitless deeds of darkness, but rather expose them." This means that it is not enough to simply not participate in sin. As Christians, we have a duty to expose and oppose sin whenever we can.

Finally, we have a duty to elect good leaders. Psalm 125:3 says, "The scepter of the wicked shall not remain over the land allotted to the righteous, for then the righteous might use their hands to do evil." Some people believe that if we would only get people saved, then all problems will evaporate. Anyone who has hung around a church very long knows that organizations composed of only saved people still have many problems. Moreover, this passage says that we cannot let wicked people rule over us or we (the righteous) will end up using our hands to do evil.

- Have your children watch a television political talk show (such as The McLaughlin Group) and discuss biblical principles related to the topic of the show.
- Attend a meeting of a local unit of government and discuss how Christians could make differences in this government if we held positions of influence.

- Find a local candidate you believe in and help him with his campaign. One ideal project would be to become a precinct captain. Together with your older children (age 12 and up), you could contact all registered voters in your precinct in three stages: (1) hand out a piece of campaign literature; (2) call or visit each home and find out if any of the adults in the home intend to support your candidate; and (3) make sure that each person you identify as intending to vote for your candidate gets to the poll on election day. If one family would take charge of each precinct in this country, there would be no election in which we could not substantially affect the outcome.

6. We should advocate the maximum freedom possibl consistent with the moral law of God.

As Christians we need to be strong supporters of our nation's commitment to freedom. However, total freedom has its problems.

While we support freedom of speech, we do not support the freedom to say, "Stick up your hands, this is a robbery. Give me your money." Nor should a person have the freedom to shout "THEATER" at a crowded fire. (You know what I mean.)

Freedom has limitations. It is popular to say that freedom is limited by the principle, "I should not have the freedom to harm another person." While this principle is fairly good, it has its limitations. This principle is widely used to support the argument that drugs should be legalized. It is argued that drug use does not affect anyone other than the user so it should be no one else's business.

So-called victimless crimes and immoral actions between "consenting adults" are justified under this system of thinking.

It is better to say that we believe in the maximum freedom possible consistent with the fundamental principles of morality reflected in the Old and New Testament. Stealing should always be wrong, even when it does little apparent harm to another. Murder should always be wrong. Drunkenness (whether induced by alcohol or drugs) should be wrong because it is immoral. This is not to say that our laws should reflect the details of the Old Testament law system. Rather, the moral principles of right and wrong should be upheld as they once were in this country.

The biblical position against abortion is predicated on the principle that it is wrong to take the life of an innocent person. We know from Scripture that unborn children are individual persons in God's eyes. Therefore, it is wrong to kill that person and the general principle of freedom must give way to the moral law prohibiting taking the life of another.

- Discuss with your children the indirect harms to others when people take drugs or participate in sexual immorality.

- Discuss the immorality of suicide.

- Discuss the passages in Scripture that clearly teach that the unborn child is a person in the sight of God. (See, for example, Luke 1:44; Psalm 139:14; Isaiah 44:2.)

7. Christians should not be treated as second class- citizens, nor should we treat others as second-class citizens.

Some liberals use the principle of "separation of church and state" to argue that Christians cannot bring their faith into the public arena. One Supreme Court decision held that the only constitutionally impermissible motive that a state legislature can have is the motive to advance Christianity.

These arguments are wrong. Everyone should have the right to participate in the process of public policy and government and to do so as a whole person. This means that Christians have the right to fully participate in citizenship activities even though our motivation for action stems from our faith.

By the same token, atheists, Buddhists, Jews, Mormons, Jehovah's Witnesses, and members of every other religion should have the same right.

This does not mean that we should wear our religious faith on our sleeve in the process of public policy. For example, it should not matter that the reason I am opposed to racial discrimination is that I believe it violates a principle in the New Testament (Col. 3: 11). All that should matter is that I oppose racial discrimination. I should have the right to reach whatever political conclusions I wish based on my whole system of thinking and beliefs, which includes my religious beliefs.

We have a special duty to stand up for the rights of other believers in other nations which do not have a commitment to the principle of religious tolerance in public affairs. (If you are interested in this subject you should contact Christian Solidarity International, a human rights organization specializing in religious freedom.)

There is a difference between saying that all religions should have equal standing before the law and saying that all religions are equally valid. I do not believe that all religions are equally true. I simply believe that it is not the business of government to determine which religious beliefs are true and which are false.

Religious freedom should be virtually absolute in this country. The only limiting factor would be when religious action is taken in a way that would violate a fundamental moral principle, such as child sacrifice or polygamy.

- Discuss the difference between civil toleration of religion by government, and the attempt to get people to believe that all religions are equally valid.

- Contact Christian Solidarity International and obtain the details of one or more cases of Christians facing persecution. Write letters of support on their behalf. CSI's address is P.O Box 70563, Washington, D.C. 20024.

- Write a letter of support on behalf of a Christian facing persecution in this country. Contact Christian

Legal Society, for an example. Their address is 4208 Evergreen Lane, Suite 222, Annandale, Virginia 22003.

- Write a letter of support on behalf of a person of a differing faith who is facing religious persecution. Christian Legal Society should be able to give you a lead on this as well.

8. Free enterprise and property rights are essential freedoms.

As Christians we tend to spend most of our energies on religious freedom and moral issues. While these issues are of unquestioned importance, we also need to be concerned about our rights associated with economics.

First of all, we should demand that our government respect the economic freedom of our children and grand-children by eliminating the national debt. In the fall of 1992, the national debt was $4 trillion. That is $16,000 for every man, woman, and child in America. A $4 trillion stack of $1000 bills would be 245 miles high. If this amount were in $10 bills it would fill three Houston Astrodomes.

Thomas Jefferson gave us a clear indication of the thinking of the Founding Fathers on the subject of government debt:

The question whether one generation has the right to bind another by the deficit it imposes is a question of such consequence as to place it among the fundamental principles of government. We should consider ourselves unauthorized to saddle posterity with our debts, and morally bound to pay them ourselves.

The preamble to the Constitution says that the purpose of the Constitution is to secure the blessings of liberty to us and to our posterity. The practice of Congress to buy today's votes to be paid for by our children and our grandchildren is simply robbery. The next generations will be forced to pay for things they will never see or use.

A related principle is that government at all levels must respect the rights of private property. Government should only be able to limit a person's use of property when the use is immoral or demonstrably harms another. A centralized, planned economy utterly failed in the Soviet Union. Our willingness to engage in half-way measures of centralized economic planning ensures us that we will remain halfway between bankruptcy and prosperity. However, with the weight of the national debt added to the tendencies toward centralized economic planning, we have gone a long way toward using the government to destroy our economy.

Politicians who campaign that they will create jobs should be viewed with deep suspicion. The only way the government can create jobs is to tax the people and employ a person to work for the government or for a contractor doing work for the government.

The best thing the government can do to create jobs is to lower taxes. Then businesses have an *incentive* to succeed. Government should also reduce regulation so that businesses have a *chance* to succeed.

- Read Larry Burkett's book, *The Coming Economic Earthquake.* Read it aloud to your older children and discuss it.

- Have your children interview a local businessman and ask him to describe regulations that control his business. Ask him to describe how his business would function if regulations he believes to be unnecessary or excessive were changed or eliminated.

- Have your children write to the Chamber of Commerce and ask what regulations a person would have to comply with to start businesses such as a restaurant, a waterslide park, or a gas station.

Chapter 7

The Treasure at the End of the Road

*B*oth parents have the duty to participate in the raising of their children at all stages of life. Mothers have some special duties in the early years. Fathers have some special duties in the later years of childhood.

Many children in our churches seem to go through a progression of starting off very well but finishing poorly. Part of this progression can be attributed to the increasing pressure of peers and the world that comes with the teenage years.

Home schooling children, however, generally not only start well but also finish well. But this is not universally true. I have begun to notice that a fair number of home schooling kids are showing some of the same symptoms of rebellion and peer dependency that characterizes the world's system—not the majority, but a fair number.

These few home schooling families see their children doing very well while they are young. They are obedient, loyal, and faithful. Then, during the teen years, there is a shift and the home schooled child begins to display some of the attitudes that typify teenage rebellion. The most likely reason for this shifting pattern of behavior is a failure by the father.

If we, as fathers, do our job well, we can be among those parents who are enjoying the glorious treasure of a child who walks maturely with God, with his family, and with his fellow man.

The educational benefits of home schooling are apparent. We can do an excellent job of providing our children with quality academic preparation for life without the problems inherent in a peer-based system of education.

But the real treasures of home schooling go beyond academics.

These treasures include raising teenagers who never experience a generation gap with you, their mom and dad. They share your values. You share life together. You learn to walk in accord. (Walking in accord is different from walking in unison. Your older children should learn to be a unique individual in God's creation while still living in harmony with the rest of his or her family.)

You have the treasure of presenting a pure daughter to be married to a godly young man. Or you may be the father of that godly young man, looking forward to the start of a new family on a sound basis.

You will have the treasure of having peace about the future your grandchildren will face. You recognize that the world will be uncertain. But you know that you have created a legacy that will enable each generation to respond with spiritual stability even as the world spins in new and troubling directions

You will have the treasure of helping to renew our nation. I am convinced that home schooled children are going to serve as leaders of our nation in numbers far disproportionate to our percentage of the population. We have raised privileged children. It used to be that children considered "privileged" were those who received a lot of money from their parents. Now the commodity in greatest demand in our society is not money but time. Your children are receiving an investment of America's scarcest resource—time. Many children given this advantage will inevitably become leaders.

More than any other, you will enjoy the treasure of seeing a spiritual revival that will stand the test of time.

We have heard much talk about revival for the past decade or so. Every political event involving Christians I have attended seems to contain calls and prayers for revival.

But there are no evidences of revival which are apparent if you look at Wall Street, Main Street, Capitol Hill—or even in our churches.

A revival is a movement that overwhelmingly turns a generation to Christ in a way that shakes up a culture.

The revivals of the past have not survived from generation to generation. One generation burns hot, the next lukewarm, the next cold.

A revival is alive in America, but it is unrecognized because people are not looking in the right places. They are not looking in the home schooling homes of this nation. As a consequence, they do not see the generation that is being turned to Christ and to mature Christian living that promises to stand the test of time. This revival will last and it will shake up our churches and it will reform our nation.

The task will not be easy. The road is clearly long. And there are many pitfalls and detours. Involved fathers are the ingredient most essential to ensure that this will be a long-term revival and not a short-term fad.

The last two verses in the Old Testament declare:

> *See, I will send you the prophet Elijah before that great and dreadful day of the lord comes. He will turn the hearts of the fathers to their children, and the hearts of the children to their fathers; or else I will come and strike the land with a curse.*

Mal. 4:5-6

Dads, we have a unique duty and opportunity. Our land will be blessed or it will be cursed, depending on us. Let us faithfully and consistently turn our hearts toward our children and secure the blessing of God for our children, our grandchildren, our nation, and our world. If we do, we'll find that the burdens along the way are far outweighed by the blessings of children who shine like brilliant stars in the sky.